For our daughters

Poem by Chélesse Edwards

(Originally published under "For my daughters" in Strut 2 and Brown Butterfly)

Artwork by Dr. Darcova Matrice

This book is dedicated to our daughters…

Ava Victoria, Autumn Marie,
Isis Omari, Mesi Dior and Paris Emani

This book is also dedicated to all of "our" daughters…
Remember that you are as unique and important as each hair that grows on your head. Your hair is beautiful and a special legacy!

It journeyed with us from the native land
Stripes on our backs…
Shackles on our hands…
Stripped of our dignity
Uprooted…
Then grounded in fear…
Couldn't get to our roots though
Because we still had our hair

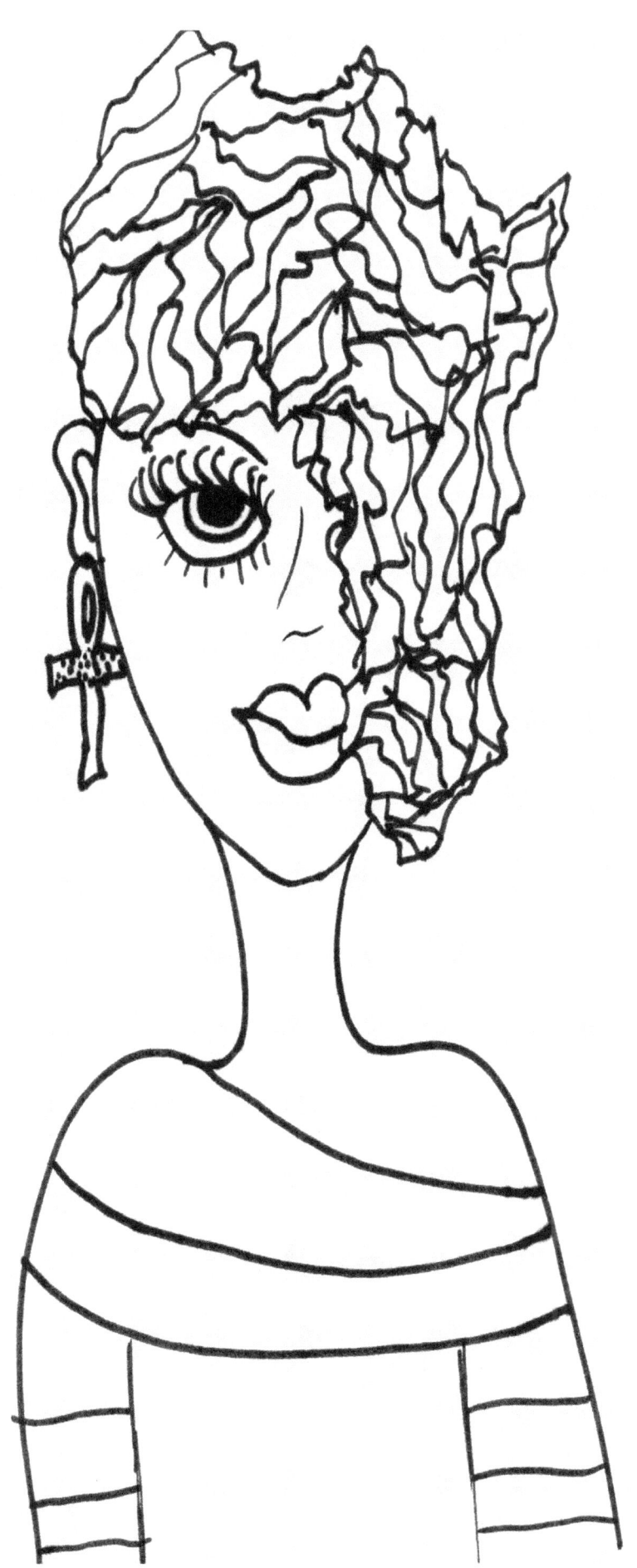

BLACK Hair...
Curled...
Coiled...
Resilient...
Always snap back hair

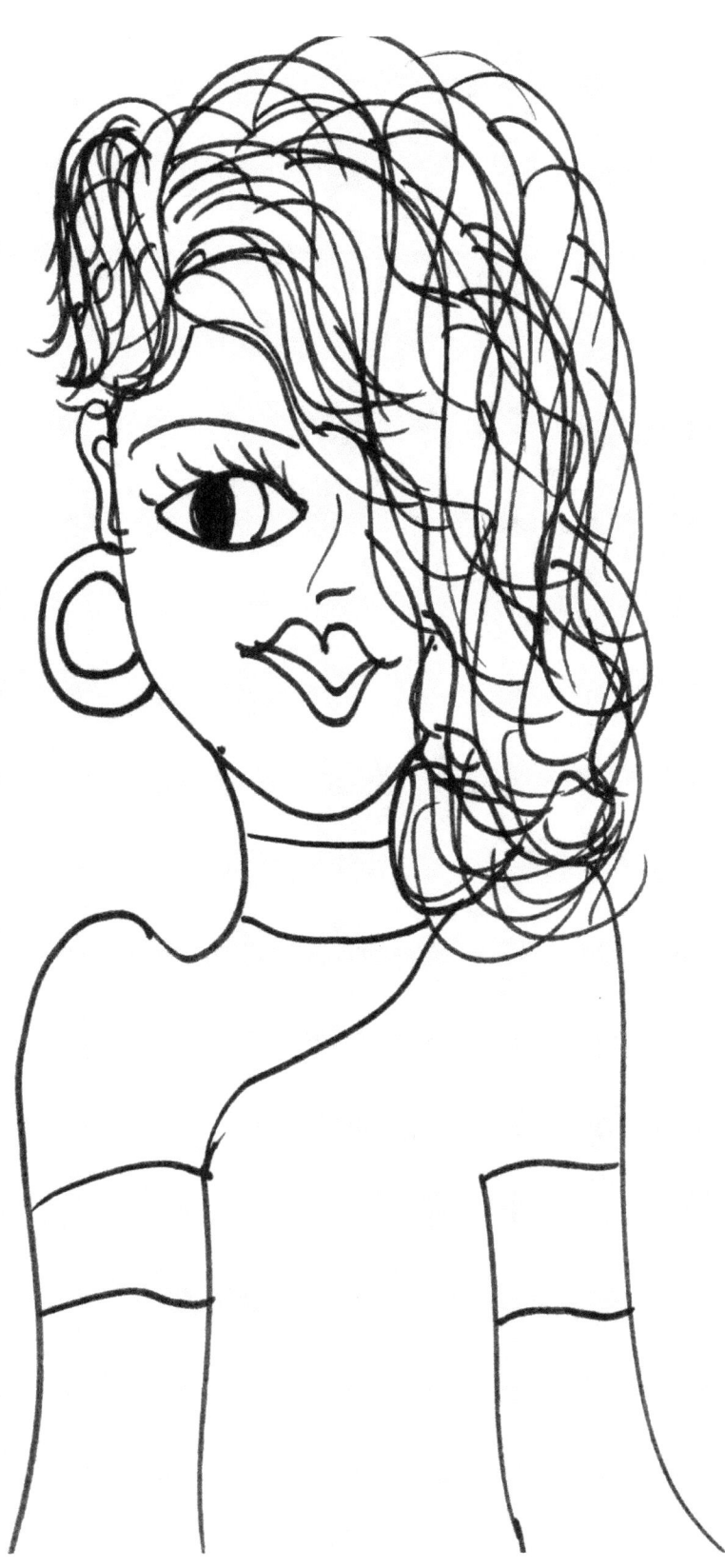

Tie it down at night
Or for waves?
Better strap a cap hair

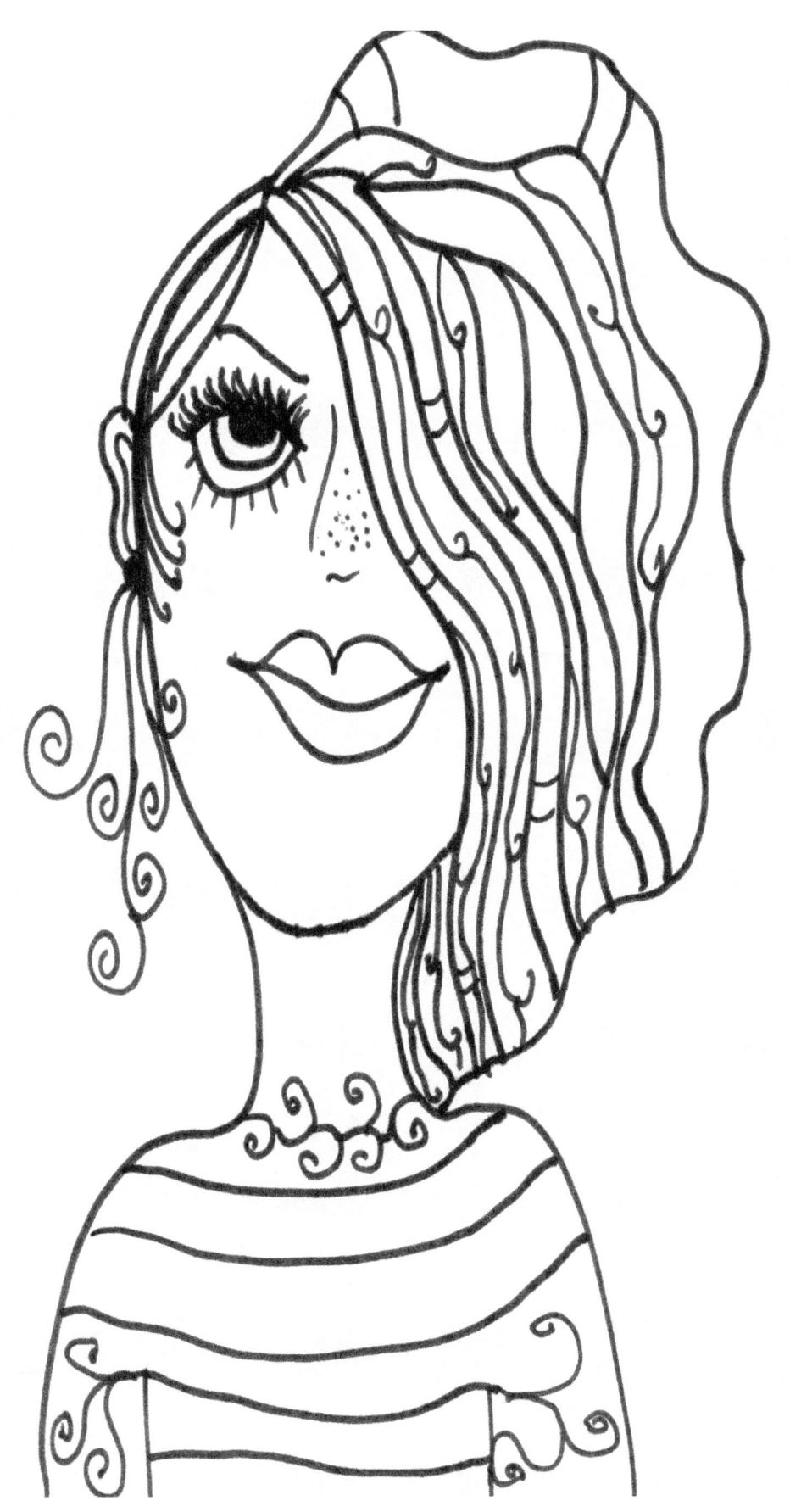

Even if you press it
It's irrepressible
Always dressable
Insanely flexible and
accessible hair

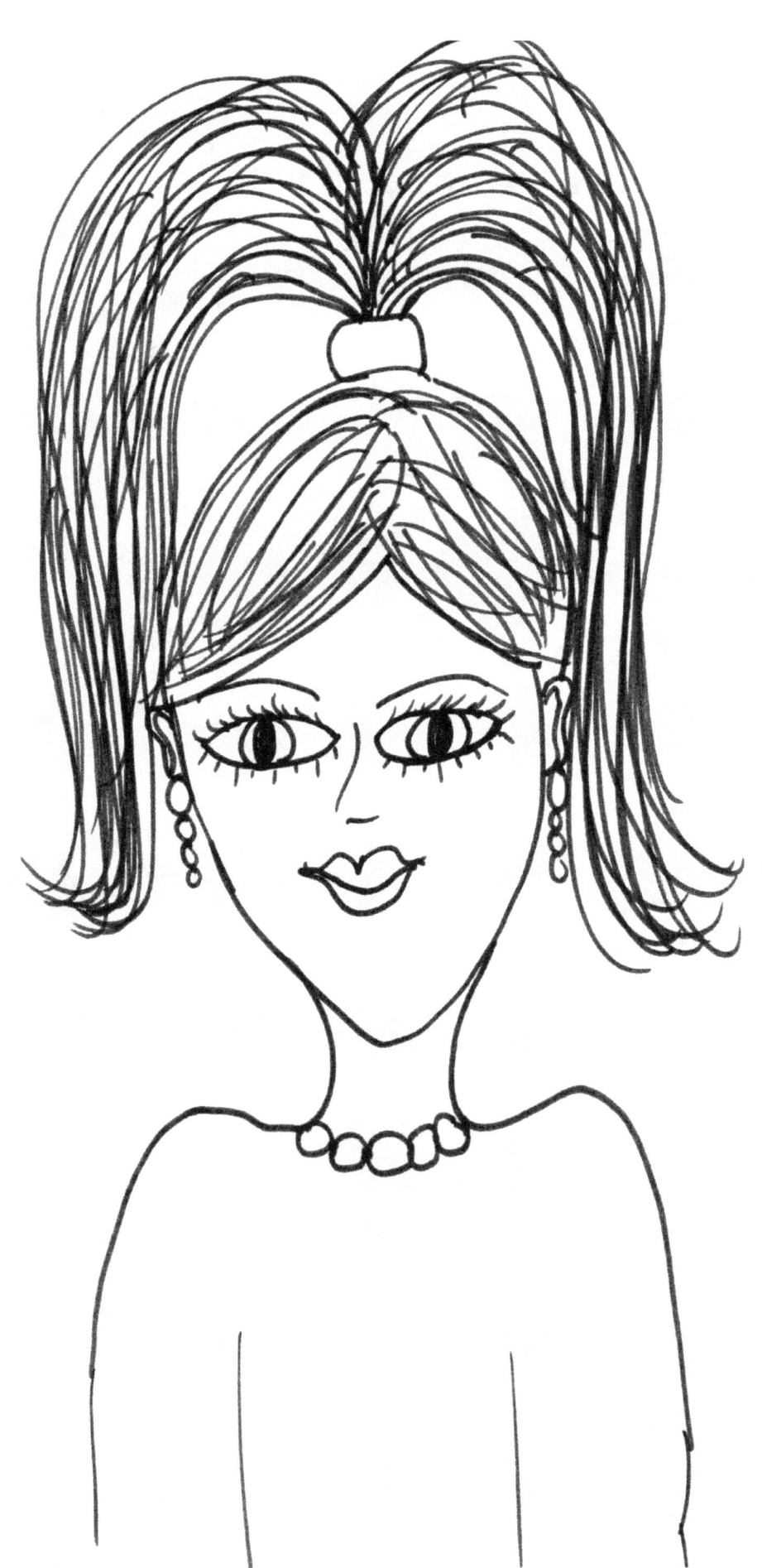

**Straight hair...
Flat hair...
All of it is black hair...**

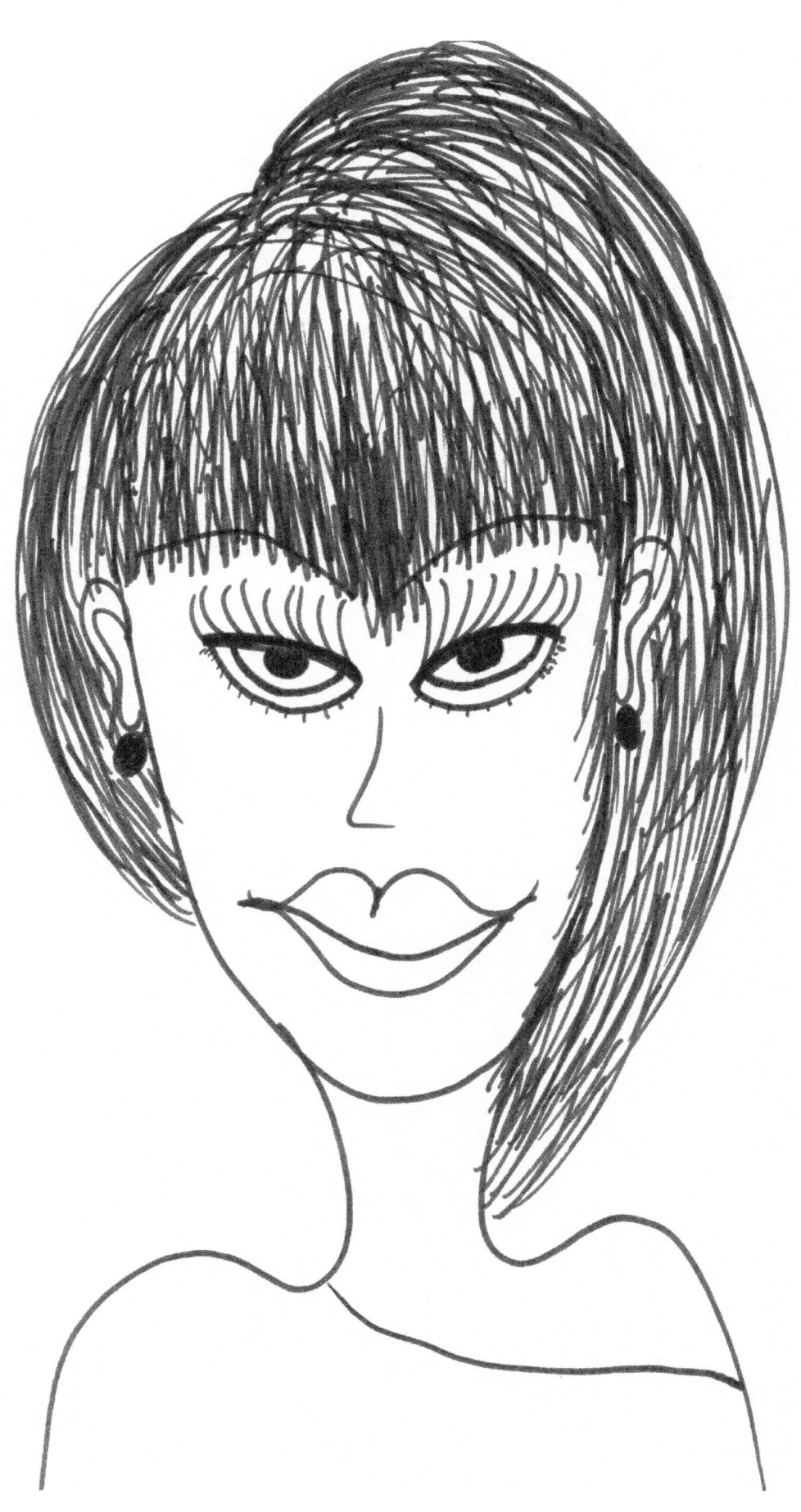

Pump it up to a flat top…
Bring it down with a fade…
Shave it off…
Then weave it up…
It's a masquerade!

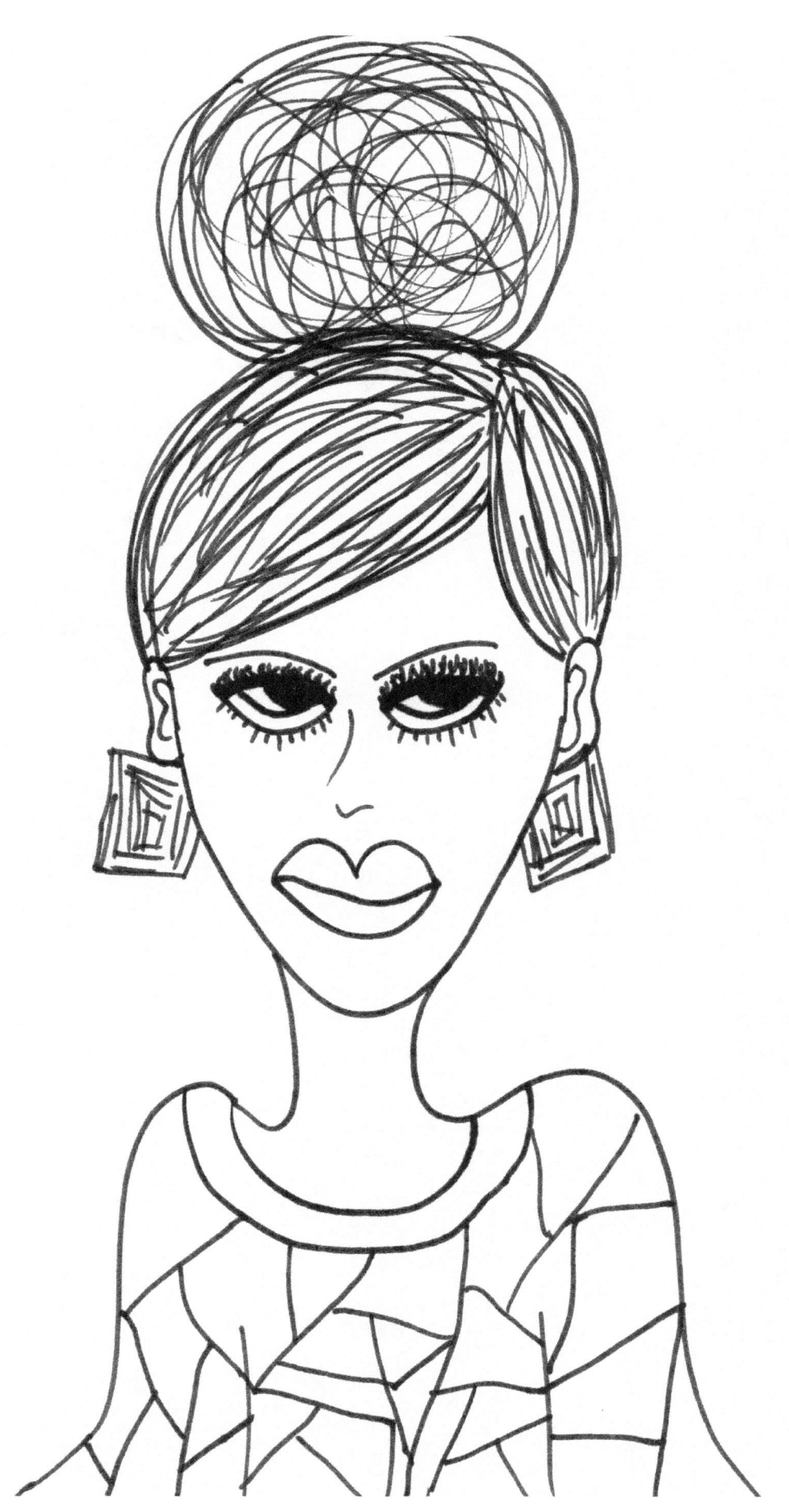

From cotton rows to corn rows...
Locked chains to locs...
I'm not fond of the Jheri curl but in the 80s it rocked

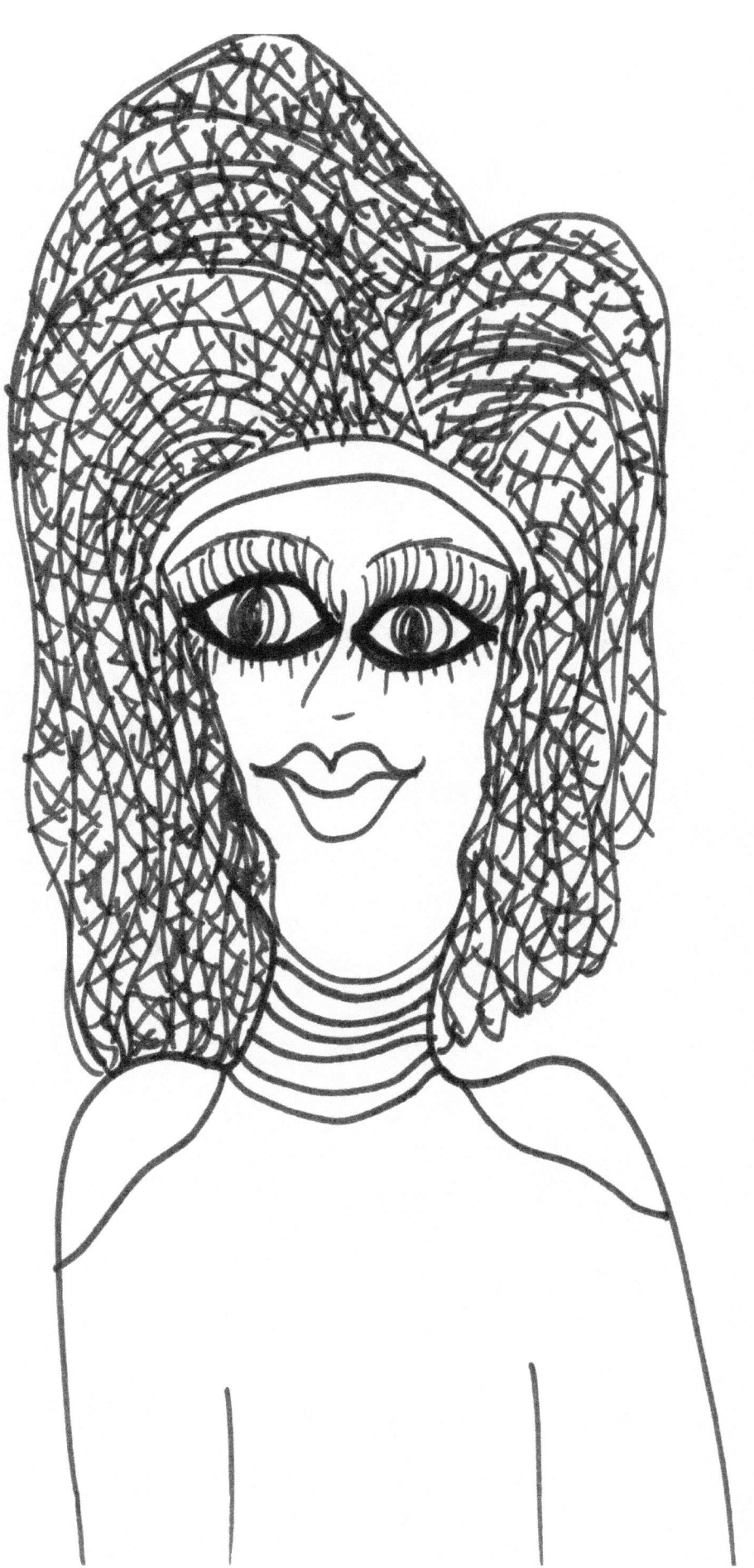

Shape it up...
Slick it back...
Wear a pony to the side...
However you represent it...
Always wear it with pride!
Think of how blessed we
are to be so diversified
with our black hair

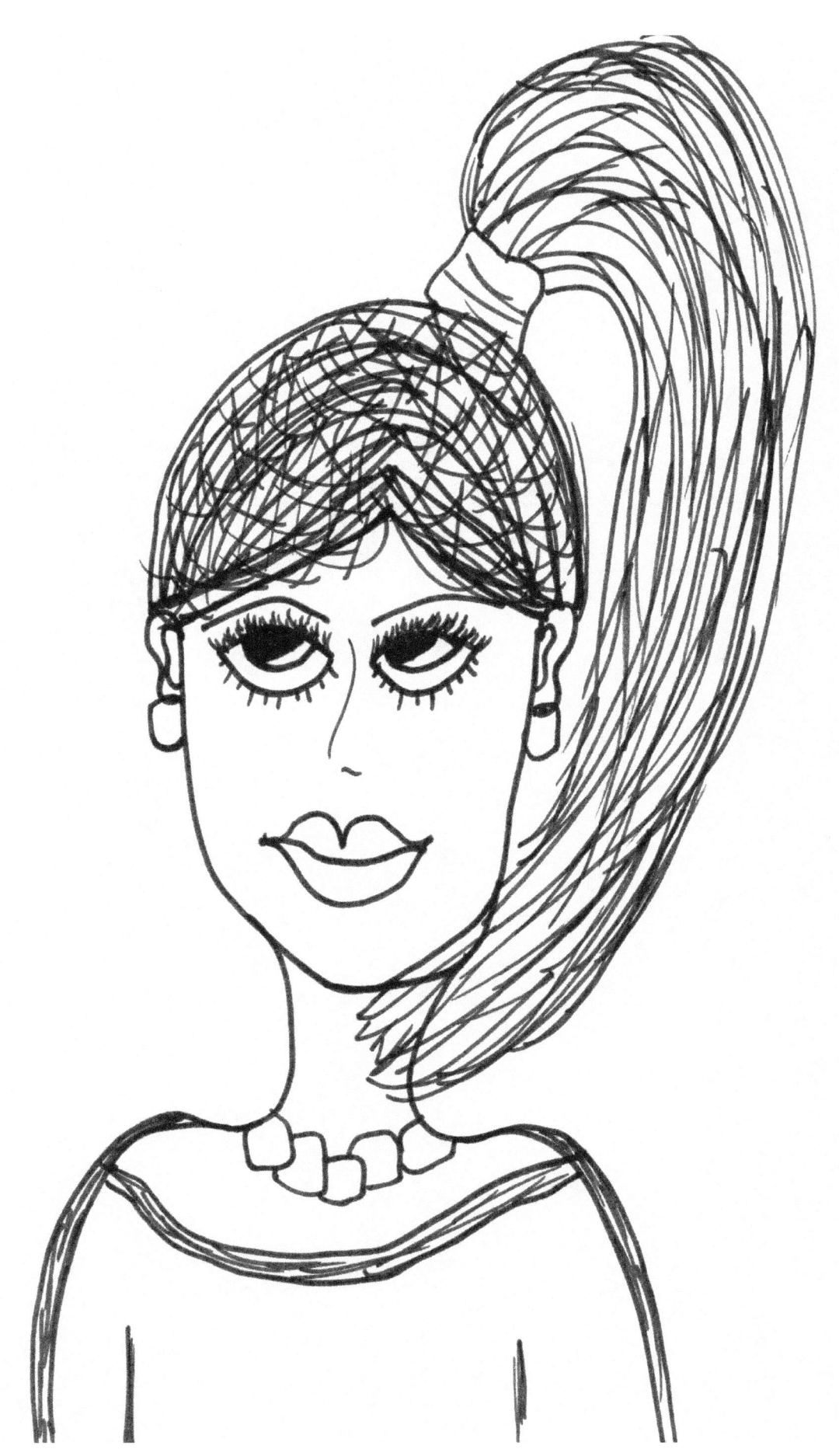

Strands of gold...
weaved together from
stories told
Little girls on mama's lap
Hair grease and bright
bows...
Beads that go
"click, clack"
Kinky's happy even when
nappy
Celebrate the facts hair

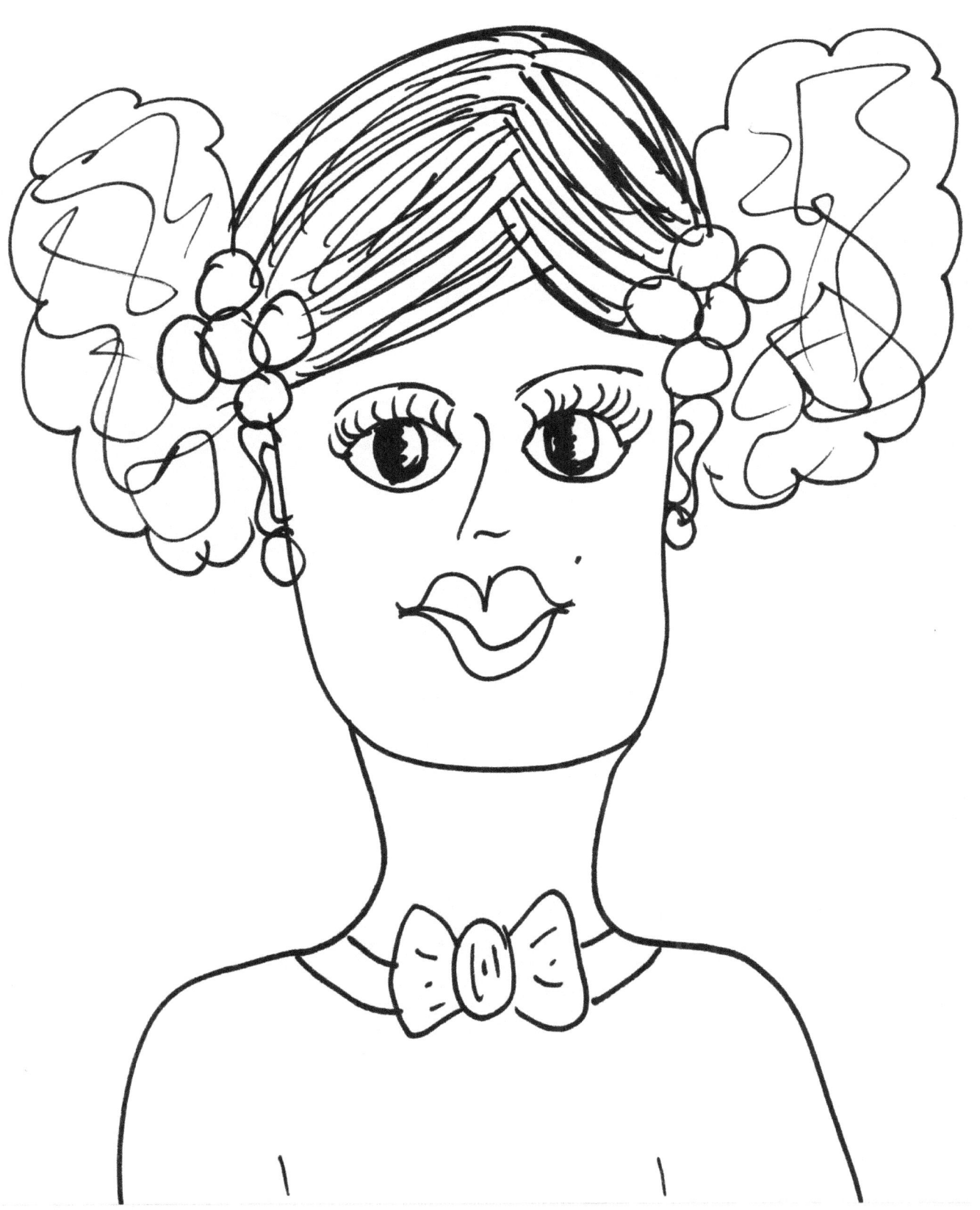

So hold up high your regal do
And think of all that we've
been through
And rejoice in our present
And be sincere because…
Every day and everywhere…
YOU grow the most sensational
Irreplaceable
Always faceable
Black hair!

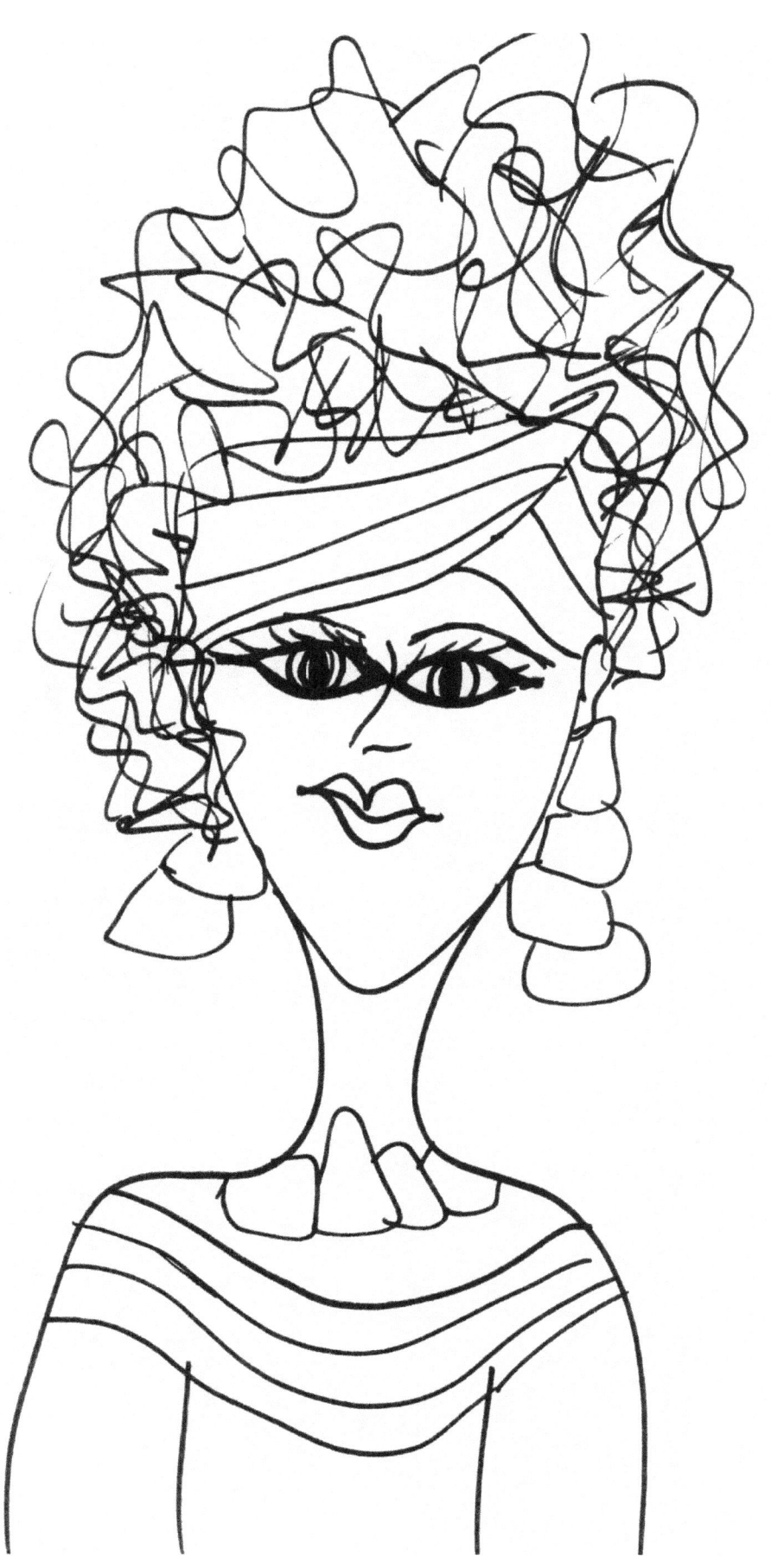

www.ingramcontent.com/pod-product-compliance
Lightning Source LLC
Chambersburg PA
CBHW081644220526

45468CB00009B/2554